BEHOLD
THE MAN!

Daily Devotions for Lent and Easter

Jeffrey Hemmer

CONCORDIA PUBLISHING HOUSE · SAINT LOUIS

INTRODUCTION

Behold the man. God is man. Jesus is the eternal Second Person of the Holy Trinity. He has existed eternally without a beginning. But then He took on flesh in the womb of His mother. And from that moment, God has had flesh—flesh just like yours, though unspoiled by sin.

In this holy Lententide, let us consider our Lord's humanity—His real body, with real body parts that perform all the real functions of a human body. We confess this Lent that Jesus, with His body, "has redeemed me, a lost and condemned person, purchased and won me from all sins, from death, and from the power of the devil; not with gold or silver, but with His holy, precious blood and with His innocent suffering and death" (Luther's explanation of the Second Article of the Apostles' Creed).

ASH
WEDNESDAY
AND THE DAYS
FOLLOWING

THE GUTS OF GOD

Read Matthew 9:35–38

When He saw the crowds, He had compassion for
them, because they were harassed and helpless, like
sheep without a shepherd. (Matthew 9:36)

Medical professionals call it the enteric nervous system. Most people call it your gut. Fascinating emerging medical research suggests that thinking with your gut, or having a gut feeling, is a real thing. Ninety-five percent of your body's serotonin—believed to regulate mood—is in your bowels. Some scientists call the gut *the second brain* because it has nearly one hundred million neurons, more than the spinal cord and the rest of the peripheral nervous system throughout the body.

In Jesus, God has guts, bowels, viscera. The Greek word for "have compassion" is *splanchnizomai*. Roughly translated, it means one's guts are moved with compassion. When Jesus has compassion, it is—quite literally—visceral. It's gut-wrenching.

And everywhere He goes, Jesus has compassion when He sees His creatures in need of His mercy, His healing, His forgiveness, His love, His Gospel, His death on the cross. He is moved to His very core—below the level of the thinking brain—for us sinners because He loves us. He has compassion on us.

God said to His belovèd Son:
   "It's time to have compassion.
Then go, bright jewel of My crown,
   And bring to all salvation.
From sin and sorrow set them free;
Slay bitter death for them that they
   May live with You forever." (*LSB* 556:5)

Lord Jesus, do not consider our sin or our unworthiness, but in Your compassion, have mercy on us and save us. Amen.

THE SKIN OF GOD

Read Genesis 3:21–24

And the LORD God made for Adam and for his wife
garments of skins and clothed them. (Genesis 3:21)

After they sinned, Adam and Eve were ashamed; their eyes were opened and they beheld their own nakedness for the first time. They sought to cover their sin with fig-leaf garments.

Their Creator then provided the pilot episode of *What Not to Wear*. He declared the garments they had made for themselves to be damnably out of fashion and incapable of covering sin and shame. Instead, God made for them the garments they needed. From skin. From an animal. The first death in the history of the universe happened at God's own hand to cover the sin of His human creatures.

Something has to die in order to cover sin. The price for sin is bloodshed.

That first animal that was killed—innocent, stripped of its skin—preaches the mercy of a God who would eventually clothe Himself in skin in order to die to cover us. Jesus shed His blood and sacrificed His life to cover the sin and shame of all mankind.

Jesus put on skin in order to cover our sin with Himself.

Make me see Your great distress,
    Anguish, and affliction,
Bonds and stripes and wretchedness
    And Your crucifixion;
Make me see how scourge and rod,
    Spear and nails did wound You,
How for them You died, O God,
    Who with thorns had crowned You. (*LSB* 440:2)

Lord Jesus, cover our sin with the robe of Your own righteousness. Amen.

THE FACE OF GOD

Read Luke 9:51–56

His face was set toward Jerusalem. (Luke 9:53)

When Moses asked to see God's glory, God only permitted him to see His back, saying, "You cannot see My face . . . and live" (Exodus 33:20). The holiness of God would destroy any sinner who beheld God's face. This is the nature of mankind's alienation from its Creator since the fall.

But in Jesus, you can behold God's face and yet live. Two thousand years ago, a few generations of people knew what Jesus' face looked like. They knew the color of His skin. They saw His face weathered by the hot Mediterranean sun. They saw His cheeks chapped by the Sea of Galilee wind. They saw His brow creased with concern. In our time and place, we don't know what Jesus' face looked like during His earthly ministry. But we do know what He did with His face.

He set it toward Jerusalem, setting His focus on giving His life for the sake of the world. Jesus' face was spit upon by sinners like us and struck by those who hated His holiness. Though He faced and suffered death, God raised Him up from the dead. Now He will never die again. We do not know what Jesus' face looks like, but we do know that His face is now before the throne of His Father, interceding on our behalf. Jesus turns His face in mercy toward those who least deserve it, and He give us peace.

> How pale Thou art with anguish,
>> With sore abuse and scorn!
> How doth Thy face now languish
>> That once was bright as morn!
> Grim death, with cruel rigor,
>> Hath robbed Thee of Thy life;
> Thus Thou hast lost Thy vigor,
>> Thy strength, in this sad strife. (*LSB* 450:2)

Lord Jesus, turn Your merciful face toward us; smile on us with Your grace and favor. Amen.

Hymn text: © 1941 Concordia Publishing House

The Forehead of God

Read Luke 22:39–46

And being in agony He prayed more earnestly; and His sweat became like great drops of blood falling down to the ground. (Luke 22:44)

"By the sweat of your face you shall eat bread," God declared to Adam (Genesis 3:19). Since God spoke this curse after the fall, even the simple task of obtaining bread from the ground has cost Adam and his descendants sweat, blood, and sometimes even life.

As the Second Adam, Jesus sweat no less than the First Adam did. While Jesus was praying in Gethsemane in great agony, He shed not only the saline perspiration of a laborer but also blood from His forehead. His capillaries ruptured, mixing blood with His sweat, a phenomenon known as hematidrosis.

The same forehead that sweat great drops of blood soon after received a crown of thorn branches woven together. Not only did this crown mock the claim that Jesus is the King of the Jews, and ultimately, the King of kings, but this crown on His forehead also intensified Jesus' suffering as He died in our place. Still He bore it. By the sweat and blood of His brow, Jesus bore Adam's sin and yours too.

> Do we pass that cross unheeding,
> Breathing no repentant vow,
> Though we see You wounded, bleeding
> See Your thorn-encircled brow?
> Yet Your sinless death has brought us
> Life eternal, peace, and rest;
> Only what Your grace has taught us
> Calms the sinner's deep distress. (*LSB* 423:2)

Lord Jesus, as You sweat and bled for my salvation, grant me relief and do not abandon me to the suffering of this life. Amen.

LENT
WEEK ONE

The Stomach of God

Read Matthew 4:1–11

And after fasting forty days and forty nights, He was
hungry. (Matthew 4:2)

The hardest part of the Lenten fast is being hungry. Enduring hunger is unnatural; it runs counter to our survival instincts.

Eating is not a sin, of course. Nor is being hungry. Fasting is not a good work. But it can serve other good works. Fasting teaches that we are not slaves of our desires. In this way, fasting can help cultivate other virtues. It teaches us that our stomach is not our god. Nor any other organ. It teaches that not every desire should be acted upon. Just as we are not enslaved to our hunger, we also are not enslaved to our sexual desires. Fasting reminds us we can respond to both kinds of desire in holy ways when they are enjoyed within God's will for His creation.

But who fasts perfectly? Who can withstand the stomach's growl? Ghrelin—the hormone that tells our bodies to eat every few hours so we don't die—occasionally wins out over our resolve.

In Matthew 4, Jesus fasted perfectly and completely for forty days. Jesus denied His stomach the food it craved, not for His sake, but for ours. We so often sin against God's holy Law by gorging our bodies on the pleasures they crave. Jesus fasted in our place and for our forgiveness.

For us baptized, for us He bore
His holy fast and hungered sore;
For us temptation sharp He knew;
For us the tempter overthrew. (*LSB* 544:3)

Lord Jesus, by Your fasting and temptation, grant us perseverance amid our disordered desires. Amen.

The Nose of God

Read Genesis 8:13–22

The LORD smelled the pleasing aroma. (Genesis 8:21)

In the Old Testament, the Hebrew idiom to describe God's anger was to say His nose grew hot (e.g., Exodus 4:14). We use a similar idiom when we say someone is red-faced with anger. Conversely, when God was pleased with someone in the Old Testament, His face would shine upon them. In fact, God's shining face, His merciful countenance, became the instrument of His blessing (see Numbers 6:24–26).

God's nose is irritated when His people rebel against Him. But it is pleased when He receives the smell of a sacrifice or incense that His people offer to Him according to His Word. He promises His people that when the smell of incense or a sacrifice reaches His nostrils, He remembers His mercy.

God does not have a nose or nostrils. The Old Testament speaks in this way to make God more understandable to those of us who do have noses. Yet, in the incarnation, the Son of God did receive a human nose, just like ours. Jesus took on our human flesh, including a human nose, so that He could become the once-for-all sacrifice that perfectly placated the Father's anger against sinners. In Jesus, we, too, are made a pleasing aroma to God (2 Corinthians 2:15).

Let my prayer rise before You as incense,
The lifting up of my hands as the evening sacrifice. . . .
Let my prayer rise before You as incense,
The lifting up of my hands as the evening sacrifice.
(*LSB*, Evening Prayer Service)

Lord Jesus, by Your perfect sacrifice, make the offerings of our prayer and praise pleasing to the Father. Amen.

The Mouth of God

Read Hebrews 1:1–4

In these last days He has spoken to us by His Son.
(Hebrews 1:2)

Before Jesus' incarnation, God communicated with His people through other people, intermediaries such as Moses, Joshua, the judges, Isaiah, Jeremiah, and the rest of the prophets. But now that Jesus has a mouth, He speaks His Word to God's people through His own mouth. No longer is an intermediary necessary. No longer is there a prophet between God and His people.

The Son of God Himself opens His mouth and speaks. Every word that comes out is the eternal, unfailing Word of God. Everywhere He goes, He proclaims the good news of the reign of God, which He Himself inaugurates.

Now that Jesus has ascended to the right hand of the Father, He speaks to us through the means He has chosen. Those who have been called to preach His Word are now His mouthpieces among us. They speak His words, not their own. Jesus opens their mouths so that we may hear Him—the eternal, unfailing Word of God.

The Lord who, born of Mary,
    Came down as man and died,
Who preached to all who listened,
    For us was crucified—
This Lord, our living brother,
    In pow'r at God's right hand,
Has chosen us to carry
    His truth to ev'ry land. (*LSB* 835:2)

Lord Jesus, continue to open Your mouth by means of Your preachers and speak Your Word to us. Amen.

The Knees of God

Read Luke 11:1–13

[Jesus] said to them, "When you pray, say: 'Father, hallowed be Your name.'" (Luke 11:2)

Jesus prayed. This is strange, when we think about it, because He is God after all—the Second Person of the Trinity. What need does Jesus have of taking time away from His work of preaching, teaching, healing, and performing miracles to withdraw to an isolated place, fall on His knees, and pray to His Father?

This is one of the mysteries of the incarnation. Jesus is fully man, and He is fully divine. Yet He prayed to God the Father. Sometimes Jesus prayed for Himself. At other times, He prayed for His disciples.

When Jesus' disciples asked Him to teach them to pray, He gave them His own prayer. He told them to approach the Creator of the universe, almighty God, by calling Him "Father." This is gutsy. Who may call God *Father*? Only God the Son. So Jesus gave His prayer to His disciples. He let them have His access to His Father.

Because of your Baptism, your prayers are the same as Jesus' prayers, and they are heard before Jesus' Father and your Father.

> For us He prayed; for us He taught;
> For us His daily works He wrought,
> By words and signs and actions thus
> Still seeking not Himself but us. (*LSB* 544:4)

Lord Jesus, carry our unworthy petitions to Your Father's throne. Amen.

THE BRAIN OF GOD

Read Genesis 9:8–17

I will remember My covenant that is between Me and
you and every living creature of all flesh. (Genesis 9:15)

Who can understand the human brain? Medical knowledge and scientific research concerning the human brain increase almost exponentially every year.

Jesus has a human brain. He has neurons and synapses, electrochemical impulses, short- and long-term memory. He, too, is reminded of things. However, when God remembers, it is not in a purely passive way, as we remember. Instead, God's remembrance is an active endeavor. He brings to mind what He wants to remember. When He remembers, He acts for the good of those He remembers.

Just as God promised to remember His everlasting covenant (e.g., Leviticus 26:42; Ezekiel 16:60), God promises to remember us for the sake of Jesus. His mind is such that nothing removes us from His merciful memory. The Father has revealed in Jesus that His mind is forever set on reconciling us to Himself (2 Corinthians 5:18–20).

You are the way; through You alone
Can we the Father find;
In You, O Christ, has God revealed
His heart and will and mind. (*LSB* 526:1)

Lord Jesus, in mercy, remember us. Amen.

The Lips of God

Read Luke 22:66–71

Then they said, "What further testimony do we need? We have heard it ourselves from His own lips." (Luke 22:71)

"From His own lips" was how the chief priests and scribes sought to condemn Jesus. His lips would not deny that He is the true Son of God.

With those lips, the infant God latched onto His mother's breast. With those lips, He kissed His earthly parents. With those lips, He preached the good news of the merciful reign of God for sinners alienated from their Creator. With those lips, He spoke forgiveness to sinners, sight to blind eyes, speech to mute tongues, sound to deaf ears, resurrection to dead people. With those lips, He taught the Word of God to thousands of people.

When Jesus stood accused before the religious leaders of His people, He willingly used His lips to seal His own death sentence. As He died on the cross, His lips proclaimed forgiveness for His murderers. Then His lips closed in death as He gave up His spirit. But they did not stay closed for long. He proclaimed His victory to the captives in hell. And then His own resurrected lips proclaimed to His disciples that He now lives forever.

His lips still speak His own forgiving words through the lips of His preachers. Someday His lips will call us from the grave, giving us a resurrected body like His to speak and sing His praise forever.

Thy lips have often fed me
With words of truth and love;
Thy Spirit oft hath led me
To heav'nly joys above. (*LSB* 450:4)

Lord Jesus, send Your preachers to speak our sins forgiven and proclaim Your Word to us. Amen.

Hymn text: © 1941 Concordia Publishing House

The Toes of God

Read Leviticus 8:22–29

Moses put some of the blood on the lobes of their right
ears and on the thumbs of their right hands and on the
big toes of their right feet. (Leviticus 8:24)

God commanded that Aaron and his sons have the blood of the
sacrifice for ordination be rubbed on their right earlobes, right thumbs,
and on the big toe of their right feet. This was because Aaron and his
sons, the priests, were appointed to hear the Word of the Lord, to ad-
minister the Israelites' sacrifices, and to enter into the Holy Place.

Jesus is our perfect and final High Priest, who enters into the Most
Holy Place, not with the blood of an animal sacrifice, but with His own
blood; He is both the sacrifice and the priest.

The toes of the God-man traveled purposefully during His life on
earth. His every step was planned and purposeful. His every step was
toward the cross. The steps Jesus' toes took were ordered so that we,
too, might stand in holiness in the Father's presence, in the Most Holy
Place, covered by the blood of Jesus.

Oh, that with yonder sacred throng
    We at His feet may fall!
We'll join the everlasting song
    And crown Him Lord of all.
We'll join the everlasting song,
    And crown Him Lord of all. (*LSB* 549:7)

**Lord Jesus, as Your steps were ordered for our salvation, so keep
us on the narrow way of salvation. Amen.**

LENT
WEEK TWO

THE BONES OF GOD

Read John 19:31–37

These things took place that the Scripture might be fulfilled: "Not one of His bones will be broken." (John 19:36)

When He was born, Jesus had 270 bones. By the time He was nailed to the cross, He likely had 206 bones because some bones eventually fuse in most adult bodies. Even after being whipped, scourged, beaten, slapped, and nailed to a cross, still He did not have a single broken bone. Not one.

The Passover lamb was to be without blemish, and not one of its bones was to be broken during the Passover preparation (see Exodus 12:5, 46). Animals offered for sacrifice were likewise to be free from blemish and defect (see Leviticus 22:17–25). Only first-rate livestock specimens were acceptable sacrifices to God.

So Jesus, too, was a healthy, whole specimen of mankind; He was not a weakling or cripple culled from the herd. And He died a real human death. He is our Passover lamb, without blemish, having wholeness in all His bones. By His sacrifice, He restores us to the wholeness of what God created us to be.

Now in the manger we may see
God's Son from eternity,
    The gift from God's eternal throne
    Here clothed in our poor flesh and bone. (*LSB* 382:2)

Lord Jesus, by the strength of Your flesh and bone, strengthen us amid our infirmities. Amen.

THE HEART OF GOD

Read Mark 7:1–23

For from within, out of the heart of man, come evil thoughts, sexual immorality, theft, murder, adultery, coveting, wickedness, deceit, sensuality, envy, slander, pride, foolishness. . . . And they defile a person. (Mark 7:21–23)

It is trendy in some circles of Christianity right now to say Jesus wants you to give your heart to Him. But He doesn't need your heart. And it's not much of an offering since He knows the quality of your heart and its toxic condition. The Great Physician's diagnosis of your heart is evident in Mark 7. Sin courses through our veins with every beat of our hearts.

Therefore, the heart of God—the heart of Jesus—should be the focus of our attention instead of our own hearts. His heart beats purely. And with every beat, He actually desires to receive your sin. He desires for His heart to stop beating for your sake because your heart is unable to cease producing its stream of filth. He desires His heart to be pierced in death so that your heart will not stop eternally in death. His heart beats so that you can be delivered from your sinful heart and rise in the resurrection with a perfected body and a sinless heart. Jesus' heartfelt desire is to give you a new heart, now through His Holy Spirit and on the Last Day in the resurrection of the dead.

Come, see these things and ponder,
Your soul will fill with wonder
    As blood streams from each pore.
Through grief beyond all knowing
From His great heart came flowing
    Sighs welling from its deepest core. (*LSB* 453:2)

Lord Jesus, cleanse me from the pollution of my flesh. Raise me to new life, new desires, and a renewed heart. Amen.

THE LUNGS OF GOD

Read Mark 15:33–39

And Jesus uttered a loud cry and breathed His last.
(Mark 15:37)

Adam's lungs were filled by the breath of God at creation. Jesus' lungs were filled with that same breath so that He, the Second Adam, might breathe new life into Adam and all mankind.

As Jesus hung on the cross dying, He was suffocating. Each breath required Him to pull and push Himself up on the nails that held Him to the cross, inflicting searing pain; each breath must have been excruciating. But this was the reason He was conceived and born as a human being, with human lungs—to breathe the same air as Adam. This was His goal: to breathe the stale air that brought death on God's creation because of Adam's sin.

He inhaled all our death and decay in order to breathe life into all of creation again. He breathed on His disciples and sent them out with His life-giving breath after His resurrection to spread the new life He had won. This new life comes through His word of Absolution, His hard-earned gift of forgiveness.

Thou camest to our hall of death,
   O Christ to breathe our poisoned air,
   To drink for us the dark despair
That strangled our reluctant breath.
   How beautiful the feet that trod
   The road that leads us back to God!
How beautiful the feet that ran
To bring the great good news to man! (*LSB* 834:3)

Lord Jesus, by Your ministers, breathe Your forgiveness on us and give us life. Amen.

Hymn text: © 1967 Augsburg Fortress. Used by permission.

THE CHEEK OF GOD

Read Matthew 5:38–42

I gave . . . My cheeks to those who pull out the beard;
I hid not My face from disgrace and spitting. (Isaiah
50:6)

Turn the other cheek (see Matthew 5:39). Everyone knows that Christian maxim. And no one practices it. People often know just enough about Jesus to completely miss who He truly is and what He came to do. It is safer to reduce Him from God Incarnate to a moral teacher, to pare down the holy God in human flesh to just another wise guru.

But Jesus' command to turn the other cheek actually is not wise. Nor is it moral. It's just foolish. It will cost you a bruised cheek. Or worse.

The cheeks of the Son of God, which were kissed by His mother Mary, were one day struck by those in the court of the high priest. He has cheeks so that He could offer them up for hateful men to strike. He is fully human so that He could turn His whole life over to the evil desire of sinners to hate and kill. And yet by His sacrifice, He assuaged the guilt of those sinners and ours too.

Thou hast suffered men to bruise Thee,
    That from pain I might be free;
Falsely did Thy foes accuse Thee:
    Thence I gain security. (*LSB* 420:5)

Lord Jesus, You bore for us the Law's condemnation. By Your suffering and death, set us free from sinful self-preservation. Amen.

The Fingerprints of God

Read Hebrews 2:14–18

He had to be made like His brothers in every respect.
(Hebrews 2:17)

By the time an unborn baby is six months old in the womb, the ridges of skin on her hands, feet, fingers, and toes bear the marks that will identify her for her entire life. Her fingerprints are unique to her alone.

Jesus, too, has unique human fingerprints. The incarnate Son of God, who is fully God and fully man, has a human body that is uniquely His—just as each of our bodies is distinct from any other human body.

But Jesus is also distinct from the rest of humanity because He is perfectly sinless. While the rest of us are self-absorbed idolaters, Christ rightly worships and obeys His Father in purity and holiness.

In the resurrection on the Last Day, our humanity will find its completed re-creation in Christ's resurrection. Presumably we will still have our fingerprints. We will retain all our individual uniqueness, but at last, we will be unsullied by sin. We will be fully human as we were created to be, as Jesus is in His resurrected body.

This great High Priest in human flesh
Was icon of God's righteousness.
His hallowed touch brought sanctity;
His hand removed impurity. (*LSB* 624:2)

Lord Jesus, preserve our uniqueness and make us like You in Your sinlessness. Amen.

Hymn text: © 1997, 2003 Chad L. Bird. Used by permission.

The Feet of God

Read Mark 10:32–34

He began to tell them what was to happen to Him,
saying, "See, we are going up to Jerusalem." (Mark
10:32–33)

Jesus does some peculiar things with His feet. After the fall, God promised Jesus' heel would crush the serpent's head (Genesis 3:15). But in order to do that, Jesus' feet walked in ordinary and extraordinary ways during His earthly ministry. Walking the dusty roads between towns in Galilee was ordinary; but walking *on* the Sea of Galilee was extraordinary. And sometimes what looked ordinary—walking to Jerusalem—was actually extraordinary. Jesus' feet traveling to Jerusalem was the greatest act of mercy we will ever know.

Many old crucifixes have a skull and crossbones at the bottom. One tradition suggests that Golgotha, the Place of the Skull, where Jesus was crucified, was the place where Adam was buried. The skull and crossbones are under Jesus' feet because, as Paul wrote, "He must reign until He has put all His enemies under His feet. The last enemy to be destroyed is death" (1 Corinthians 15:25–26).

As Jesus died, defeated death was put under His feet. His death destroyed death. For Adam and all his descendants, death has been placed under Jesus' feet—destroyed, powerless.

Calv'ry's mournful mountain climb;
>   There, adoring at His feet,
Mark that miracle of time,
>   God's own sacrifice complete.
"It is finished!" hear Him cry;
Learn from Jesus Christ to die. (*LSB* 436:3)

Lord Jesus, remind us of Your crushing victory over death and give us hope in the resurrection. Amen.

THE VOCAL CORDS OF GOD

Read Mark 2:1–12

[Jesus] said to the paralytic, "Son, your sins are forgiven." (Mark 2:5)

The scribes actually were right: "Who can forgive sins but God alone?" (Mark 2:7). But they were dead wrong in assuming the man who spoke to the paralytic could not forgive sins simply by what He said. "Why does this man speak like that?" Because that man—Jesus—was and is God.

Forgiveness is the language of God, His native tongue. Therefore, Jesus, the Word of God in human flesh, speaks forgiveness. He could command the paralytic to get up and walk home with as little difficulty as He could speak sins forgiven.

He has vocal cords for this function: to speak sinners forgiven. From His first cry when He emerged from His mother's womb to His final cry on the cross, every sound of Jesus' voice was for this purpose: to forgive sins.

After His resurrection, one of the first things Jesus did was breathe the Holy Spirit on His disciples and give them His voice: "If you forgive the sins of any, they are forgiven them" (John 20:23). His voice became theirs. His forgiveness became theirs to speak.

"Come unto Me, ye weary,
    And I will give you rest."
O blessed voice of Jesus,
    Which comes to hearts oppressed!
It tells of benediction,
    Of pardon, grace, and peace,
Of joy that hath no ending,
    Of love that cannot cease. (*LSB* 684:1)

Lord Jesus, by Your authority over sin and death, speak us forgiven and deliver to us eternal life. Amen.

LENT
WEEK THREE

THE FINGER OF GOD

Read Luke 11:14–23

But if it is by the finger of God that I cast out demons,
then the kingdom of God has come upon you. (Luke
11:20)

When Jesus drove out demons, some marveled. But others suspected He could not have that much power unless He had teamed up with demonic forces. They said, "He casts out demons by Beelzebul, the prince of demons" (Luke 11:15).

In one sense, they were right. There is no middle ground. Jesus can only do what He does—drive out demons, heal the sick, raise the dead—either by the power of Satan or by the finger of God.

The finger of God is an expression that shows up even in the Egyptian magicians' perception of Yahweh's actions during the plagues (see Exodus 8:19). But with Jesus, the phrase means even more than the people in Luke 11 seemed to understand. Jesus' finger *is* the finger of God. With His finger, He drives out demons. With His finger, He plunders Satan's kingdom and breaks the devil's stranglehold on us.

His finger still works among us, touching us in His holy Sacraments, showing us that the kingdom of God has come upon us also.

Your touch then, Lord, brought life and health,
    Gave speech and strength and sight;
And youth renewed and frenzy calmed
    Revealed You, Lord of light.
And now, O Lord, be near to bless,
    Almighty as before,
In crowded street, by beds of pain,
    As by Gennes'ret's shore. (*LSB* 846:2)

Lord Jesus, by the finger of God, deliver us from the devil's reign. Amen.

The Hair of God

Read Matthew 10:26–33

Even the hairs of your head are all numbered. Fear
not . . . ; you are of more value than many sparrows.
(Matthew 10:30–31)

Before you read this devotion, take a minute (or 1,440 minutes) and count the number of hairs on your head. I'll wait.

How'd you do? Did any fall out while you were counting? Are you sure you got them all? What about the ones on your neck? Did you count those?

It's okay if you weren't exactly successful. Any reasonable person knows it's a futile endeavor.

Yet, without any estimating or speculating, the God who made the heavens and the earth does know the precise number of hairs on your head—a fact about yourself you cannot and will not ever know.

The Creator cares so much for you He sent His own Son to have a head full of hairs, just like you. He cares for your every need enough to meet even your most pressing need—your alienation from Him. Jesus came among us as one of us to die in order to reconcile us to His Father.

You are of more value than many sparrows. How much are you worth? Worth is determined by what another person is willing to pay. Jesus paid for you with His life. You are worth the life of God.

My faith would lay its hand
   On that dear head of Thine,
While as a penitent I stand,
   And there confess my sin. (*LSB* 431:3)

**Lord Jesus, as You know the number of hairs on our heads,
teach us to entrust all our cares to Your gracious provision. Amen.**

THE EYES OF GOD

Read Luke 19:41–48

When He drew near and saw the city, He wept over it.
(Luke 19:41)

The human eye is amazing in its intricacy. Light passes through the cornea as the camera-shutter iris governs the amount of light allowed to enter. The light then passes through the lens, which changes its shape to alter the focus. The lens focuses the light through the vitreous humor, a gel-like substance that fills the eye, and projects the light onto the retina, upside down. The retina transforms light rays into electric impulses, transmitting them over a million nerve fibers via the optic nerve. The optic nerve relays the information to the brain. Finally, the brain puts all the information together into a picture, flips it rightside up, and creates an image of what is seen.

The incarnate Son of God has human eyes that, like our eyes, often caused His heart and mind to be stirred by what He saw. What Jesus saw, the picture in His brain, on His way into Jerusalem on Palm Sunday broke His heart. In Jerusalem, the city where God chose to place His name and to meet with His people in mercy, Jesus saw the signs that God's people were rejecting Him, their Savior. And Jesus' eyes wept for the people and for Jerusalem.

Often have Your eyes, offended,
　　Gazed upon the sinner's fall;
Yet upon the cross extended,
　　You have borne the pain of all. (*LSB* 423:1)

Lord Jesus, look in mercy upon us Your people, and keep Your cross ever before our eyes. Amen.

THE CLOTHES OF GOD

Read John 19:23–24

When the soldiers had crucified Jesus, they took His garments and divided them into four parts. (John 19:23)

After Adam and Eve sinned, they grasped at fig leaves to cover their nakedness; their eyes were suddenly turned inward, and they felt ashamed. In mercy, God made clothes of animal skins for them. And ever since, the descendants of Adam and Eve have worn clothing.

Jesus came among us as the incarnate God, Himself clothed with the flesh of man. And like sinners hiding behind the safety of clothing, Jesus, too, wore clothes.

Yet part of the humiliation of crucifixion was being stripped naked before being hung on a cross. At Jesus' death, He had no shame from His own sin. But as the sin-bearer, naked and exposed to the eyes of the mocking crowds, Jesus bore the shame of every sinner.

The clothes of the Son of God were gambled away at His death, leaving Him with no possessions. But in losing everything, He gained everything—including you. He was stripped so that He could clothe you with the perfect garment of His own righteousness. All who have been baptized are clothed with Jesus, who covers all sin and shame.

Your blood my royal robe shall be,
    My joy beyond all measure!
When I appear before Your throne,
Your righteousness shall be my crown;
    With these I need not hide me.
And there, in garments richly wrought,
As Your own bride shall we be brought
    To stand in joy beside You. (*LSB* 438:4)

Lord Jesus, preserve for us the robe of Your righteousness, which You delivered in Holy Baptism. Amen.

THE THROAT OF GOD

Read Hebrews 9:15–22

Under the law almost everything is purified with blood,
and without the shedding of blood there is no forgiveness of sins. (Hebrews 9:22)

In the tabernacle and later in the temple, sacrifices were offered
every day. The priests sacrificed the hooved animals by slitting their
throats and draining the animals' blood out. Every day.

Sometimes the blood drained from the animal's throat was poured
on the altar; sometimes it was poured out over the people. What the
writer of Hebrews says about blood and forgiveness was not metaphorical for God's people in the Old or New Testaments. Sacrifices were
bloody. The ritual God gave His people for the forgiveness of their sins
was gory.

The priesthood and sacrifices God gave to Israel were always
meant to point to the perfect, once-for-all sacrifice of the Son of God,
the Lamb of God, who is both sacrifice and final high priest. His throat
was not slit; but His side was pierced, His blood was drained, and His
throat did preach and still preaches an eternal, limitless forgiveness,
obtained by His own blood.

But Christ, the heav'nly Lamb,
>   Takes all our sins away;
A sacrifice of nobler name
>   And richer blood than they. (*LSB* 431:2)

**Lord Jesus, by Your perfect sacrifice, declare all our sins forgiv-
en. Amen.**

THE SIDE OF GOD

Read John 19:33–35

Christ loved the church and gave Himself up for her,
that He might sanctify her, having cleansed her by the
washing of water with the word. (Ephesians 5:25–26)

God made Eve from Adam's side while Adam was in a deep sleep. Adam and Eve's origin shows the relationship God intended them to have: "Therefore a man shall leave his father and his mother and hold fast to his wife, and they shall become one flesh" (Genesis 2:24).

When Jesus died on the cross, a soldier pierced Jesus' side with a spear, and out of the Second Adam's side came blood and water. The water from Jesus' side pools in the baptismal font. From the water that flowed from His side, He creates the Church—His Bride. Baptism joins sinners—dead in their sins and alienated from God—to Christ as His holy Bride. The blood from Jesus' side flows into the Communion chalice, and there Jesus' Bride is united to Him forever through His forgiveness and eternal life.

The mystery of a man and woman united in marriage is profound, but it points to the wonderful, mysterious, eternal union of Christ and His Church. What God has joined together, He will never separate. His Bride, for whom He died, is His forever.

Crown Him the Lord of love.
    Behold His hands and side,
Rich wounds, yet visible above,
    In beauty glorified. (*LSB* 525:3)

Lord Jesus, by Your Means of Grace, join us into Your one holy Church. Amen.

THE EARS OF GOD

Read Psalm 28:1–9

Blessed be the LORD! For He has heard the voice of my
pleas for mercy. (Psalm 28:6)

The ears—not the eyes—are the organs of faith. "Faith comes from
hearing" (Romans 10:17). Faith is not in what is seen but in what is
unseen (see Hebrews 11:1). The art of the Christian life is learning to
believe our ears more than our eyes. Our eyes see a dying world, but
our ears hear the promise of resurrection for all creation. Our eyes see
our sins, but our ears hear the Lord's declaration that in Christ we are
holy and pure. Our eyes see persecution of the Church and martyrdom
of Christians, but our ears hear Jesus' promise that the gates of hell
cannot prevail against His Church.

Jesus' ears hear in two directions. As God, His ears are attuned to
the prayers of His people. As man, His ears are attentive to what God
the Father says. Jesus hears and perfectly obeys His Father's word and
will. And Jesus hears and perfects the petitions of His people, bringing
their prayers to His Father.

Even now, Jesus hears. He lives to hear and to intercede for His
Church. He still has ears. He still hears.

By Thy helpless infant years,
By Thy life of want and tears,
  By Thy days of deep distress
  In the savage wilderness,
By the dread, mysterious hour
Of the insulting tempter's pow'r,
  Turn, O turn a fav'ring eye;
  Hear our penitential cry! (*LSB* 419:2)

Lord Jesus, hear our unworthy prayers and bring them to Your
Father's throne. Amen.

LENT
WEEK FOUR

The Teeth of God

Read Luke 22:14–23

He said to them, "I have earnestly desired to eat this
Passover with you before I suffer." (Luke 22:15)

In the Garden of Eden, Adam and Eve ate what God had prohibited. In rebellion, they sank their teeth into the forbidden fruit.

The last meal Jesus sank His teeth into before His suffering and death was a Passover meal. Yet as the One who fulfilled the purpose of the Passover meal, He gave a new command that night to whoever believes in Him: "Take, eat" (Matthew 26:26). The bread He gave His disciples that night was the fruit from a different tree—the tree of the cross. That bread was His body, offered as an atoning sacrifice for all sins. That bread is still His body when it is fed to us in Holy Communion.

Jesus took the curse earned by Adam and Eve's rebellious eating and instead gives us the gracious invitation to come and eat. To come and eat His very own body so that we may live.

It takes a God with teeth—a God who has become man—to redeem mankind, who by eating became sinners.

One last paschal meal to eat,
One last lesson as their teacher,
Washing Your disciples' feet. (*LSB* 445:2)

Lord Jesus, devour our ancient enemy death. Amen.

Hymn text: © 1991 Concordia Publishing House

The Circumcision of God

Read Luke 2:21–38

At the end of eight days, when He was circumcised, He was called Jesus. (Luke 2:21)

God gave circumcision as the sign of His covenant with Abraham and all of Abraham's descendants (see Genesis 17:1–14). Therefore, it is significant that Jesus was circumcised on the eighth day of His life, as God had commanded Abraham. In fact, this is so significant, a whole day has been set aside in the Church Year—January 1—to commemorate the circumcision and naming of Jesus.

Why does it matter that Jesus was circumcised? Because those who were truly part of God's people, Israel, sought to live according to God's Law. And for males, that included being circumcised. Jesus was circumcised because He came to fulfill what God's people, Israel, did not and could not do—Jesus was perfectly obedient to the Law, the perfect Son in Israel's place (see Hosea 11:1).

At Jesus' circumcision, the Holy Spirit spoke through Simeon and Anna to reveal that the few drops of blood shed on the eighth day of Jesus' life pointed ahead to the stream of His blood that would flow from His cross for the salvation of the world. Through Israel's one true and faithful Son, God has reconciled us all to Himself and has made us all His children.

> His infant body now
>> Begins the cross to feel;
> Those precious drops of blood that flow
>> For death the victim seal. (*LSB* 898:3)

Lord Jesus, by Your perfect obedience, atone for our failure to live faithfully as God's redeemed children. Amen.

THE SOUL OF GOD

Read Luke 23:44–55

Jesus, calling out with a loud voice, said, "Father, into Your hands I commit My spirit!" And having said this He breathed His last. (Luke 23:46)

Only humans possess souls. So for Jesus to be fully human, He must possess both a body and a soul, as we do. His humanity—body and soul together—began when He was conceived in His mother's womb. And His humanity now continues eternally.

Jesus declared that no one could take His life from Him; He laid it down by His own authority (John 10:18). After brutal torture, Jesus gave up His spirit on the cross; in that moment, His soul and body were rent asunder as unnaturally as when any other person dies.

When Jesus rose, He was neither a disembodied soul nor a soulless body. He rose a man—His body and soul were knit back together. And on the day of His return, He will bid you rise in the same way—to a perfect and restored existence of your body and soul together for eternity.

Jesus, all Your labor vast,
All Your woe and conflict past,
Yielding up Your soul at last:
    Hear us, holy Jesus. (*LSB* 447:19)

Lord Jesus, preserve us in body and soul until the day when You raise us to live forever in You. Amen.

The Mother of God

Read John 19:25–27

Standing by the cross of Jesus were His mother and
His mother's sister, Mary the wife of Clopas, and Mary
Magdalene. (John 19:25)

Jesus spoke to His mother from the cross. Mary is obviously the mother of Jesus. But can we call her the mother of God?

What did she bear in her womb? What does the Nicene Creed say? This man, begotten of the Father from all eternity, is "God of God, Light of Light, very God of very God, begotten, not made, being of one substance with the Father, by whom all things were made; who for us men and for our salvation came down from heaven and was incarnate by the Holy Spirit of the virgin Mary and was made man."

Mary is the mother of the man named Jesus. And this man is truly God. Thus, not only is it correct to call Mary the mother of God, but it is also necessary to do so. In Jesus, God and man are inseparably united. Thus, God has a mother. This does not glorify Mary; it glorifies her Son. Even as an unborn zygote, blastocyst, embryo, and fetus, Mary's Son was God. As a baby, a toddler, a boy, an adolescent, a young man, He was God. As a man dying on a cross, He was still fully and completely God. The Son of God has a mother because He fully became one of us.

Jesus, loving to the end
Her whose heart Your sorrows rend,
And Your dearest human friend:
    Hear us, holy Jesus. (*LSB* 447:7)

Lord Jesus, by Your incarnation, remember us who need You in all stages of human life. Amen.

THE NAME OF GOD

Read Matthew 1:18–21

*An angel of the Lord appeared . . . saying, . . . "[Mary]
will bear a son, and you shall call His name Jesus, for He
will save His people from their sins." (Matthew 1:20, 21)*

Jesus is the Greek form of the Hebrew name *Joshua*, which means "the Lord saves." Never has a name been more appropriate, more fitting, or more descriptive.

Jesus Himself did not mince words about why He had come: "I came not to call the righteous, but sinners" (Matthew 9:13).

As a pastor, I often tell my parishioners we should put a sign over the doorway to the church building saying "Only sinners welcome." That may cut against the grain of American do-it-yourself salvation schemes, but it's a true statement. Jesus is not the Savior of the righteous. He is the Savior of sinners.

Never shy away from confessing your sins. If your sins are only peccadillos from which you can easily save yourself, you have no need of a Savior. But if you have sins—big sins, sins from which you cannot free yourself, sins that rightly earn you death and hell—then you truly need a Savior, and you can rejoice that His very name proclaims that He came for the purpose of saving you from your sins. All of them. Eternally.

Jesus! Name of priceless worth
To the fallen of the earth
For the promise that it gave,
"Jesus shall His people save." (*LSB* 900:3)

Lord Jesus, Savior of sinners, have mercy on us sinners. Amen.

THE BEARD OF GOD

Read Isaiah 50:4–9

I gave . . . My cheeks to those who pull out the beard.
(Isaiah 50:6)

A sure way to torture a person is to pull out his hair. How much more so when the hair is pulled out of a person's face. No man in his right mind would allow someone to pull out his beard if he could do anything to prevent it. In the ancient world, nearly all men allowed their beards to grow; therefore, a man whose beard had been pulled out had been forcefully subjected to someone else's power and will. It was a sign of disgrace and shame.

But Isaiah spoke of the Suffering Servant who would allow the unthinkable: He would allow others to pull out His beard.

Other men suffer the humiliation and agony of someone pulling out their beard against their will. But this Suffering Servant is the Son of God. He has power and dominion over all things. If anyone is going to pluck out the beard of God, it will only happen because He gives Himself up to this excruciating torment. Jesus was willingly obedient even to the point of a horrible death. He did it to rescue you eternally from pain and death.

Thou hast suffered great affliction
    And hast borne it patiently, . . .
Thou didst chose to be tormented
That my doom should be prevented. (*LSB* 420:6)

Lord Jesus, by Your willingness to endure crucifixion for us, embolden us to face the struggle against our sinful flesh and to live in Your holiness. Amen.

The DNA of God

Read Hebrews 4:14–16

Since therefore the children share in flesh and blood,
He Himself likewise partook of the same things, that
through death He might destroy the one who has the
power of death, that is, the devil. (Hebrews 2:14)

The Human Genome Project was the first comprehensive attempt to sequence the entire human genome, the DNA of a human's twenty-three chromosomes, containing more than three billion pairs of nucleotides. It took thirteen years with researchers at twenty universities in six different countries to complete the project, and it cost close to $3 billion. Now, sixteen years later, you can have your genome sequenced for a few hundred dollars or less. You spit into a plastic tube and mail it to a lab; the results can tell you where your DNA is unique, where you are predisposed to certain diseases, why you have a widow's peak or a second toe that protrudes past your big toe, or what kind of diet is best suited to your genetics.

Whatever this field of biology, which is still in its infancy, can tell us about ourselves and about what we may be predisposed to experience or do, what we know for sure is that Jesus' DNA is perfect, uncorrupted by sin. God gave us our DNA as part of our creaturely existence, and one day our DNA will be like Jesus'—still unique, but perfected. There will no longer be mutations or distortions. We will be God's re-created creatures.

The royal banners forward go;
The cross shows forth redemption's flow,
Where He, by whom our flesh was made,
Our ransom in His flesh has paid. (*LSB* 455:1)

Lord Jesus, restore us to the very core of our beings. Amen.

LENT
WEEK FIVE

The Head of God

Read Hebrews 2:5–11

We see Him who for a little while was made lower than the angels, namely Jesus, crowned with glory and honor because of the suffering of death. (Hebrews 2:9)

The same head into which a crown of thorns was pressed, mocking one who had been called a king, now is crowned with the eternal diadem of Him who reigns over the whole cosmos.

For thirty-three years, Jesus doffed His crown. He set aside the power and privilege that are rightfully His. He willingly made Himself nothing (see Philippians 2:6–8) and accepted His Father's will, which would lead to thorns, nails, and a cross as well as shame, scorn, rejection, and death.

He was obedient to His Father's will in order to gain the crown of life for us. Therefore, His head, which once was despised and gory, now is rightly crowned with all glory and honor. His head, with our same skin and blood, truly is also the head of God, deserving to bear the mark of His almighty power and dominion. And yet He chose for His head to bear the mark of His love for us—the mark of His suffering, which made us children of the King.

O sacred Head, now wounded,
    With grief and shame weighed down,
Now scornfully surrounded
    With thorns, Thine only crown.
O sacred Head, what glory,
    What bliss, till now was Thine!
Yet, though despised and gory,
    I joy to call Thee mine. (*LSB* 450:1)

Lord Jesus, we thank You that, by wearing the crown of thorns, You have secured for us the crown of eternal life. Amen.

THE CHEST OF GOD

Read Mark 9:33–37

If anyone would be first, he must be last of all and
servant of all. (Mark 9:35)

C. S. Lewis once warned that the trajectory of modern education would form metaphorically chestless men. The chest mediates between a person's head and belly, between their thinking and their desires. People governed purely by their bellies are hedonists; they can only act for their own pleasure. People governed purely by their heads are useless; they cannot act.

But the chest in between is an important part of being human. It guides a human being's actions with the heart, stirred by compassion and virtue. Jesus, fully man, has both the metaphorical chest C. S. Lewis talked about and a physical, anatomical chest. Jesus has the virtue that seeks to give up His life for the good of all mankind. And He has the warmth and affection to invite little children to come to Him.

This virtue and compassion in Jesus' metaphorical chest took Him to the cross. He denied His belly's instinct to avoid pain. He was not trapped in the intellectualism of only knowing what God desired and never doing it. His whole being—His physical and metaphorical chest, as well as His head and belly—was fully given to the selfless sacrifice of His life for the life of the world.

Hosanna, loud hosanna,
> The little children sang; . . .
To Jesus who had blessed them,
> Close folded to His breast,
The children sang their praises,
> The simplest and the best. (*LSB* 443:1)

Lord Jesus, deliver us from the affliction of being ruled by our passions. Amen.

The Cells of God

Read Psalm 139:13–24

You knitted me together in my mother's womb. (Psalm 139:13)

Every person begins as a single cell, a zygote. This single-celled human being nevertheless has a full complement of DNA, unique to that microscopically small person. On the first day of that person's life, the cell doubles through mitosis. By the fifth day of a human's life, the ten to thirty cells of a morula become a blastocyst, and the cells begin rapid mitosis, growing to numbers of two hundred or three hundred. Biologists estimate an adult human has 37.2 trillion cells.

Not every person survives from a single-celled zygote to a multi-trillion-celled adult. And no one dodges death forever. But every death is unnatural, contrary to our Creator's design for His creation. Yet even though our cells die, whether in small ways during our lifetime or in a big way when we stop breathing and our whole body dies, death does not have the final word about our existence.

Jesus is fully and completely human. From a single cell, He eventually grew to be a multitrillion-celled man. Though there is wide diversity in the functions adult human cells perform, every one of Jesus' cells existed for a single purpose: to die on the cross. His life, death, and resurrection redeem all of us, even to the smallest cell.

He sent no angel to our race,
Of higher or of lower place,
But wore the robe of human frame,
And to this world Himself He came. (*LSB* 544:2)

Lord Jesus, by Your death and resurrection, You offer the hope of resurrection to all people and the promise of restoration to all creation. Amen.

The Tongue of God

Read Psalm 22:1–24

My tongue sticks to My jaws; You lay Me in the dust of death. (Psalm 22:15)

The tongue is a peculiar organ. It comprises eight different muscles and is the only muscular hydrostat in the human body. As the primary taste organ, it is covered with thousands of taste buds that die and re-grow every few weeks. The tongue allows us to swallow, shape sounds into words, and breathe effectively.

On the cross, when Jesus had not eaten or drunk for hours, His tongue acutely felt His suffering. On the cross, the psalmist's description of suffering was fulfilled by Jesus. His strength was dried up like a potsherd, a broken fragment of kiln-fired pottery; His mouth was thirsty and dry, His tongue sticking to His jaws and the roof of His mouth.

His suffering, including His excruciating thirst, brought our redemption. And now He lives so that His tongue can proclaim through His Word and through those He sends the forgiveness He has won for all people.

Jesus, in Your thirst and pain,
While Your wounds Your lifeblood drain,
Thirsting more our love to gain:
   Hear us, holy Jesus. (*LSB* 447:13)

Lord Jesus, continue to speak Your words of absolution to us. Amen.

The Emotions of God

Read Philippians 1:3–11

God is my witness, how I yearn for you all with the
affection of Christ Jesus. (Philippians 1:8)

Centuries before Jesus' birth, philosophers were struggling to
understand human emotions. Hippocrates speculated that a person's
health, including emotions, was governed by the interplay of four hu-
mors: black bile, yellow bile, phlegm, and blood. Aristotle connected
emotions to a person's quest to live virtuously. Today, there are numer-
ous theories about human emotions. We know there are cognitive and
physiological elements: the brain perceives stimuli, hormones are re-
leased, and the body has a physical, even visible, response to the stimuli and hormonal triggers. But in many ways, the complexity of our
emotions still mystifies us.

Jesus has emotions, just like we do. He wept at the death of His
friend Lazarus. He had affection for Jerusalem. He had compassion. He
became angry. He experienced anxiety and turmoil. He is zealous for
the salvation of His people.

Jesus' fervent desire that everyone would receive forgiveness and
be reconciled to God led Him to the cross. His emotions still bind His
Body, the Church, together today, just as Paul wrote to his brothers and
sisters in Philippi.

He was little, weak, and helpless,
Tears and smiles like us He knew;
And He feels for all our sadness,
And He shares in all our gladness. (*LSB* 376:3)

Lord Jesus, let Your desire for the salvation of sinners be our
zeal too. Amen.

The Veins of God

Read Acts 20:17–28

The church of God, which He obtained with His own blood. (Acts 20:28)

Humans have a closed circulatory system. Blood is never intended to leave the circuit of heart, arteries, veins, and capillaries. When it does, something is wrong.

But the body has a remarkable capacity to heal itself. When a blood vessel ruptures, platelets begin to fill the wound in order to create a scab and stop the bleeding. The body performs a series of enzyme reactions to convert soluble fibrinogens into the insoluble fibrin proteins that cause clotting, meshing around the platelets to create the scab. This process, hemostasis, keeps the circulatory system closed: blood inside, pathogens outside. The body also produces new blood, replacing lost platelets every day and replenishing up to a liter's worth of red blood cells every six to eight weeks. It's a beautifully functioning system that is intended to stay closed.

Yet Jesus became incarnate in order for His circulatory system to be opened, to pour forth its contents, to shed His blood as payment for the sinful rebellion of mankind against its Creator. His blood for ours.

Glory be to Jesus,
    Who in bitter pains
Poured for me the lifeblood
    From His sacred veins! (*LSB* 433:1)

Lord Jesus, I thank You that from Your sacred veins, You poured the payment to ransom me from sin and death. Amen.

THE HEEL OF GOD

Read Genesis 3:14–15

I will put enmity between you and the woman, and between your offspring and her offspring; He shall bruise your head, and you shall bruise His heel. (Genesis 3:15)

What a promise!

But who understands this? Adam and Eve had no offspring at the time God spoke these words. And heel bruising? Head bruising? Before their fall into sin, the man and his wife had not experienced bruising and striking. The promise is the opposite of what had recently transpired.

There had been no enmity between the serpent and the woman, so she had welcomed him into their idyllic existence. But when the serpent twisted the Word of God and accused God of lying, Adam and Eve should have crushed the serpent's head. Instead they entertained his insidious inquiry.

So the promise that Eve's offspring would deliver a head-crushing blow to the deceiver would undo what was done in the Garden of Eden. Eve's offspring would suffer a temporarily fatal strike to His heel. But through the ultimate blow He landed to the serpent's head, He caused death and sin to come undone.

Long on earth the battle rages,
　　Since the serpent's first deceit;
Twisted God's command to Adam,
　　Made forbidden fruit look sweet.
Then the curse of God was spoken:
　　"You'll lie crushed beneath His feet!" (*LSB* 521:3)

Lord Jesus, You crushed Satan's power. Keep the deceiver away and guard us from his temptations. Amen.

Hymn text: © Peter M. Prange. Used by permission.

LENT
WEEK SIX

THE KNUCKLES OF GOD

Read 1 Corinthians 15:20–28

The last enemy to be destroyed is death. (1 Corinthians 15:26)

Concerning the Gospel for the First Sunday in Advent, Luther said, "This King [riding into Jerusalem] is and shall be called sin's devourer and death's strangler, who extirpates sin and knocks death's teeth out; he disembowels the devil and rescues those who believe on him from sin and death."[1]

This King knocks death's teeth out. But Jesus uses more than His knuckles to render death edentulous and impotent in this cosmic boxing match. The blow Jesus delivers to the sinister snarl of death is landed with His whole body. When death sinks its teeth into Him, it is forever rendered toothless and broken. It no longer bites. Its snarl is reduced to a vapid sputtering.

Jesus delivered a blindside right hook that death could never have seen coming: He destroyed death by His death. Death is the consequence for sin, meted out only to sinners. But then Jesus, the sinless Son of God, the perfect man, died. He has won the victory for us over the last and final enemy.

> Amen, Lord Jesus, grant our prayer;
> Great Captain, now Thine arm make bare,
>   Fight for us once again!
> So shall Thy saints and martyrs raise
> A mighty chorus to Thy praise
>   Forevermore. Amen. (*LSB* 666:4)

Lord Jesus, fight for Your Church, whom You saved by Your own death. Amen.

---

1 Martin Luther and Eugene F. A. Klug, *Sermons of Martin Luther: The House Postils*, vol. 1. (Grand Rapids: Baker Books, 1996), 27.

The Back of God

Read Isaiah 52:13–53:12

Surely He has borne our griefs and carried our sorrows.
(Isaiah 53:4)

Marred. Despised. Rejected. Acquainted with grief. Bore our griefs. Carried our sorrows. Stricken. Smitten by God. Afflicted. Pierced for our transgressions. Crushed for our iniquities. Oppressed. Led to slaughter. Taken away. Cut off out of the land of the living. Put to grief. Poured out His soul to death. Numbered with transgressors.

That is quite a heavy load that was laid on Jesus' back.

He bore physical beatings, a scourging from the Roman soldiers that lacerated and shred His skin.

But there was a deeper scourging. The Lord laid on Him the iniquity of us all. The heaviest load, the crushing burden, the stripes which wounded deeper than any whip was the load of all the sins of men. Every sin of every person was placed on Jesus' back.

And yet that is such good news for us. He was pierced for our transgressions. He was crushed for our iniquities. Upon Him was the chastisement that brings us peace. With His wounds, we are healed. His back alone is strong enough to bear our sins. Let Jesus shoulder the load of your sins. He already has borne them all because He loves you.

Thou hast borne the smiting only
　　That my wounds might all be whole;
Thou hast suffered, sad and lonely,
　　Rest to give my weary soul. (*LSB* 420:3)

Lord Jesus, we thank You that You were crushed so that we might be healed. Amen.

The Arms of God

Read Mark 10:13–16

He took [the children] in His arms and blessed them.
(Mark 10:16)

The prophets foretold that God would roll up His sleeves and bare His own arms to fight for His people (see Isaiah 52:10; Deuteronomy 1:30). Mary's Magnificat proclaimed that that is exactly what God was doing in the person of her Son, Jesus, the incarnate Word of God. By coming among us to save, He was bringing down the mighty from their thrones and exalting those of humble estate (see Luke 1:46–55).

In the person of Jesus, God rolled up His sleeves and bared His arms against the enemies of His people. Yet His arms did not throw the punches we'd expect; He did not pick up a sword and head into battle. Instead, He welcomed children with His arms. He brushed up against lepers. He lifted the dead. He did also overturn tables and drive out the moneychangers with a whip. But the perfect and ultimate display of His limitless strength was when He stretched out His arms on the cross and let Himself be killed. This is the God who fights for us. And He has won.

Sheep that from the fold did stray
    No true shepherd e'er forsaketh;
Weary souls that lost their way
    Christ, the Shepherd, gently taketh
In His arms that they may live:
Jesus sinners doth receive. (*LSB* 609:3)

Lord Jesus, with Your strong arm, save Your people who have put their trust in You. Amen.

THE SHOULDERS OF GOD

Read John 19:16–18

He went out, bearing His own cross. (John 19:17)

Shoulders are for carrying. Even the action *to shoulder* means to carry a heavy burden or pick up a load. That is what shoulders are for. The human body is remarkably capable of carrying more than two- or three-times its own weight on the shoulders.

But Jesus bore on His shoulders far more than that. In carrying His cross, He bore the weight of every sinner, the load of the world's sin. All of it.

This is no feat for the *Guinness Book of World Records*. This is not the lore of Atlas. Jesus literally bore the weight of all human sinfulness on Himself. And He did so willingly. This was His mission, the reason He was born.

He has human shoulders in order to be able to bear the sins of mankind, to bear even your sins. No one else can do it; no one else can carry this load. The weight of your sin crushed Him. But He is strong enough that He rose up again after destroying sin. And He is strong enough to raise you up also in His new life on the Last Day.

To us a Child of hope is born,
    To us a Son is giv'n,
And on His shoulder ever rests
    All pow'r in earth and heav'n,
    All pow'r in earth and heav'n. (*LSB* 412:3)

Lord Jesus, by Your incarnation, carry for us the weight of our sins. Amen.

The Hands of God

Read John 13:1–20

[He] began to wash the disciples' feet and to wipe them with the towel that was wrapped around Him. (John 13:5)

As the children's song teaches us, Jesus does in fact have the whole world in His hands. He is the eternal Word of God, the Word through whom all things were made (John 1:1–14).

But on the night He was betrayed and handed over to those who wanted to kill Him, the One who has the whole world in His hands stooped down and took His disciples' dirty feet into His hands.

Not even the humblest task, the most servile posture, was beneath Jesus. Though He is truly God, He used His human hands to honor the men who in a matter of hours would desert Him and leave Him to die all alone. Jesus removed not only the dirt from the feet of His disciples but, with His hands nailed to a cross, He also removed the stain of sin for all who believe in Him. On the cross, He used His hands to honor all men.

As He humbly knelt before them,
 Dusty feet to wash and dry,
By His tender touch expressing
 True compassion from on high. (*LSB* 446:2)

Lord Jesus, cleanse us from our sins today and each day in the forgiveness You deliver in Your Church. Amen.

Hymn text: © 2001 Stephen P. Starke, administered by Concordia Publishing House

The Blood of God

Read Hebrews 9:11–22

He entered once for all into the holy places . . . by
means of His own blood, thus securing an eternal
redemption. (Hebrews 9:12)

Here's a simple lesson in economics: something is only worth what someone will pay for it. No matter what you think your house is worth, if no one will pay that amount, it's not actually worth whatever you imagine.

So what are you worth? What would someone pay for you? What is just one human life worth?

In the most preposterous economic exchange ever, the life of God was spent for your life. The catechism says He has redeemed you, "a lost and condemned person, purchased and won [you] from all sins, from death, and from the power of the devil; not with gold or silver, but with His holy, precious blood and with His innocent suffering and death" (Luther's explanation of the Second Article of the Apostles' Creed). All for the purpose of gaining you as His own.

He paid for you with His blood, each drop more valuable than all earthly treasure. He paid an infinite, inestimable price for you. Because to Him, you are worth the life of God.

Grace and life eternal
In that blood I find; . . .
Lift we, then, our voices,
Swell the mighty flood;
Louder still and louder
Praise the precious blood! (*LSB* 433:2, 6)

Lord Jesus, I thank You that no price was such that You would not pay it to redeem me. Amen.

The Dead Body of God

Read John 19:38–42

God the Father's only Son Now is buried yonder. (*LSB* 448:1)

In the committal rite, we pray, "O Lord Jesus Christ, by Your three-day rest in the tomb, You hallowed the graves of all who believe in You, promising resurrection to our mortal bodies. Bless this grave, that the body of our brother/sister may sleep here in peace until You awaken him/her to glory, when he/she will see You face to face and know the splendor of the eternal God" (*LSB Agenda*, p. 128).

Even as His body rested in the stone-cold sleep of death, Jesus worked. His rest hallowed all our graves. The graves we will one day be buried in are also in Christ because Jesus also rested in a tomb.

There is no need to fear death. Do not fret over the grave in which your body will one day lie. It is just a sleeping place, a temporary abode. Though death seems so permanent and powerful, the grave will yield to the authority of the One who rested in His own grave before rising to life again. He will call you forth from your grave and will knit your body and soul back together eternally. So, until then, you are safe in Christ, even when you rest in death. Jesus will surely awaken you to eternal life for you belong to Him.

Jesus, my Redeemer, lives;
　　Likewise I to life shall waken.
He will bring me where He is;
　　Shall my courage then be shaken?
Shall I fear, or could the Head
Rise and leave His members dead? (*LSB* 741:2)

Lord Jesus, give us courage to face death, trusting Your victory over death to render the grave powerless. Amen.

THE RISEN BODY OF GOD

Read Isaiah 25:6–9

Apparently the work of redeeming men from their sin by giving Himself as the full and final sacrifice left Jesus with quite the appetite.

Did you notice how nearly everywhere the risen Christ went, He was eating? He joined His Emmaus disciples for an evening meal. When He appeared to the disciples in the locked upper room, He asked them for something to eat. They gave Him a piece of broiled fish, and He ate it. When He appeared to His disciples while they were fishing on the Sea of Galilee, He greeted them with some breakfast He had cooked on a fire.

Ghosts don't eat. Jesus was not an apparition. Jesus ate after His resurrection because He was and is—as He has been since His incarnation—truly man.

We, too, will be raised on the Last Day to re-created, fully human bodies. "The LORD of hosts will make for all peoples a feast of rich food, a feast of well-aged wine" (Isaiah 25:6). Jesus has swallowed up death by His death and His rising again. Therefore, on the day of His return, we will share with Him the rich feast of the victory of the Lamb, who has completely devoured death, leaving no leftovers.

At the Lamb's high feast we sing
Praise to our victorious King. (*LSB* 633:1)

Risen Lord Jesus, nourish us with Your Word and Sacraments until we see You face-to-face at Your great and victorious wedding feast. Amen.